Calmondo

Bibliografische Information der Deutschen Nationalbibliothek:
Die Deutsche Nationalbibliothek verzeichnet diese Publikation in der Deutschen
Nationalbibliografie; detaillierte bibliografische Daten sind im Internet über
http://dnb.dnb.de abrufbar.

Take a break! Coloring Book For Grown-Ups (For Colored Pencils)
1. Auflage Oktober 2016
© 2016 Dirk Schwenecke
Herausgeber: Calmondo, Dirk Schwenecke
Autor: Dirk Schwenecke
Illustrationen & grafisches Konzept: Dirk Schwenecke
Herstellung und Verlag: BoD – Books on Demand, Norderstedt
ISBN: 9783741290015

COLORING BOOK
for grown-ups

Take a break!

This book is dedicated to my best ....

Take a break!

Step 1
Write down 5 sources of stress that you definitely need to switch off for now.

1. ....
2. ....
3. ....
4. ....
5. ....

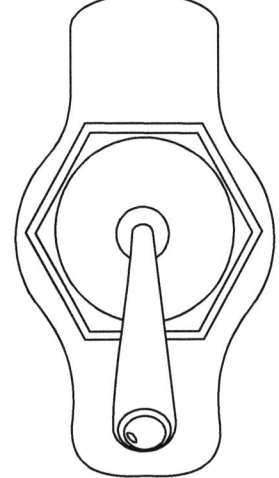

Step 2
Then get all of the tools you need to use the book.

☐ colored pencils ☐ scissors  ☐ sharpener   ☐ ruler   ☐ rubber

colored pencils
Black is no colour

scissors
Please avoid the temptation to stab something with them

sharpener
Caution! Don't flip out when you are about to run out of lead

ruler
For stressed out

rubber
To remove the shame of colouring outside the lines

Step 3
Now test your pencils and colour in the circles

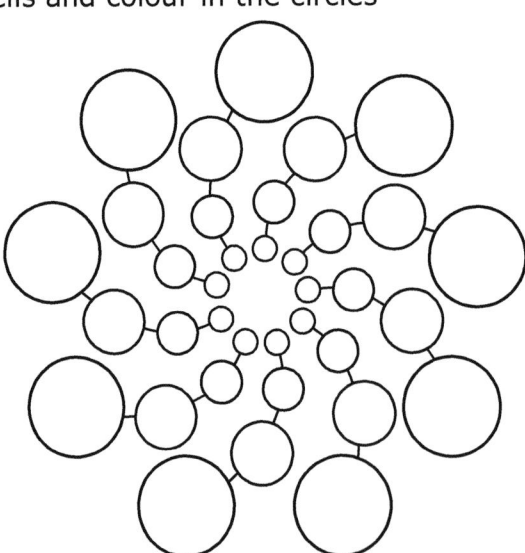

Eye examination for women!

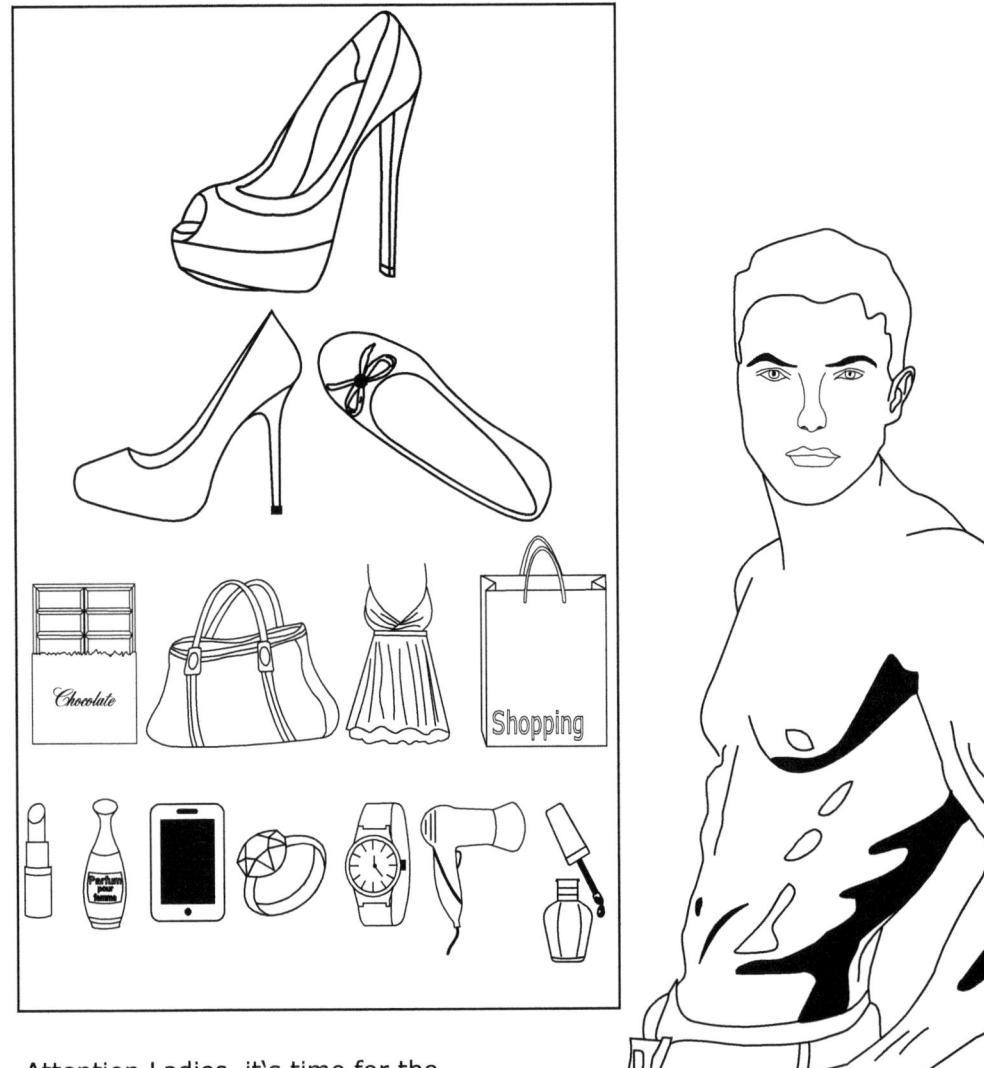

Attention Ladies, it's time for the ophthalmologist. Today we have selected a real special exemplar for you.
Can you pass the test without looking at the handsome guy.
Test it preferably with a friend or colleague!

Hit or Shit?

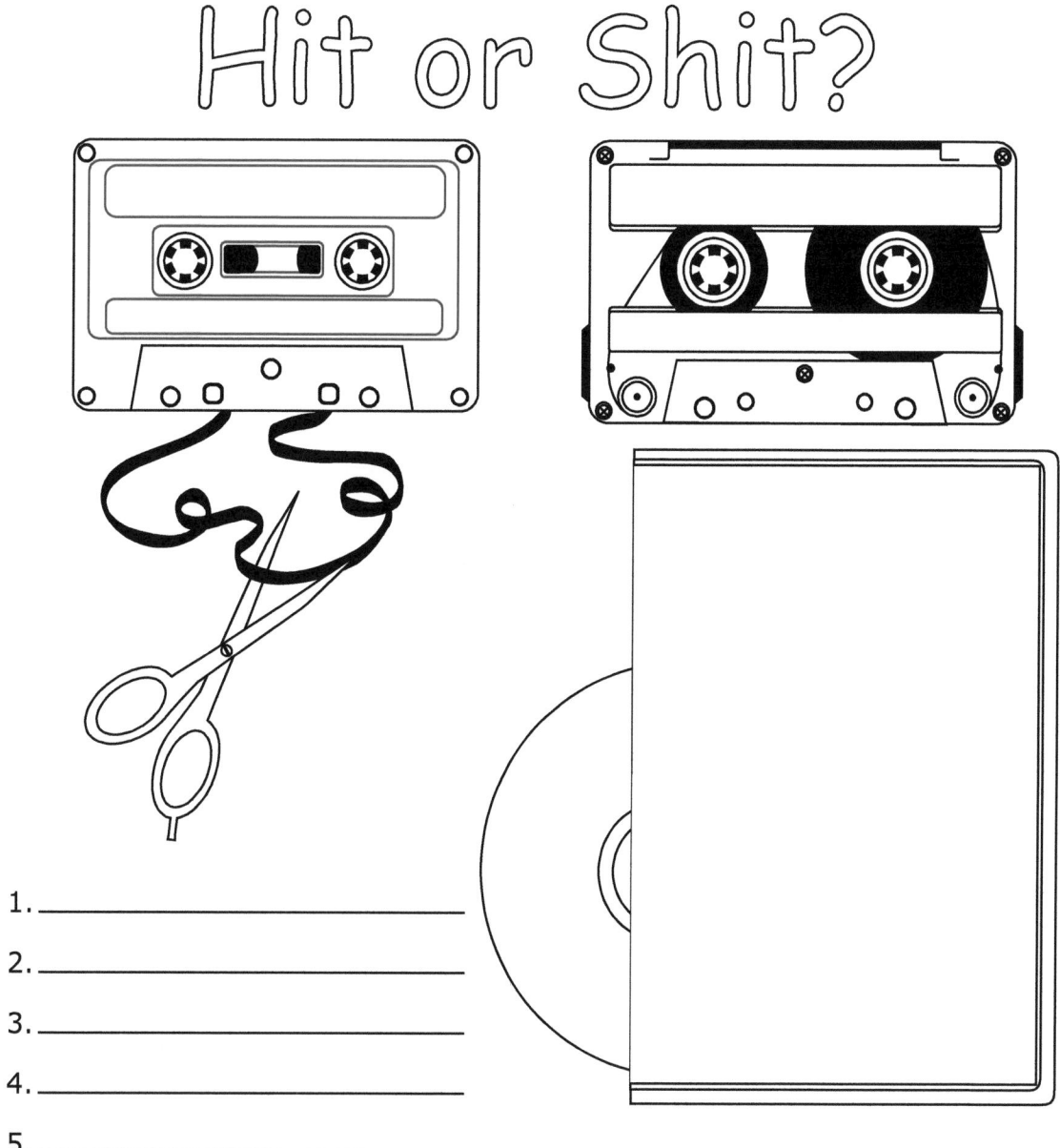

1. _____
2. _____
3. _____
4. _____
5. _____

You used to sit for hours in front of the radio, waiting for your all-time favourite songs, so that you could quickly press RECORD to record the song for eternity on your cassette. But what songs are still your favourites and ought to be burned onto a CD and which have become an absolute embarrassment and you now know are pure SHIT? Write the top 5 no-go's on the left and then design the cover on the right with your personal hits.

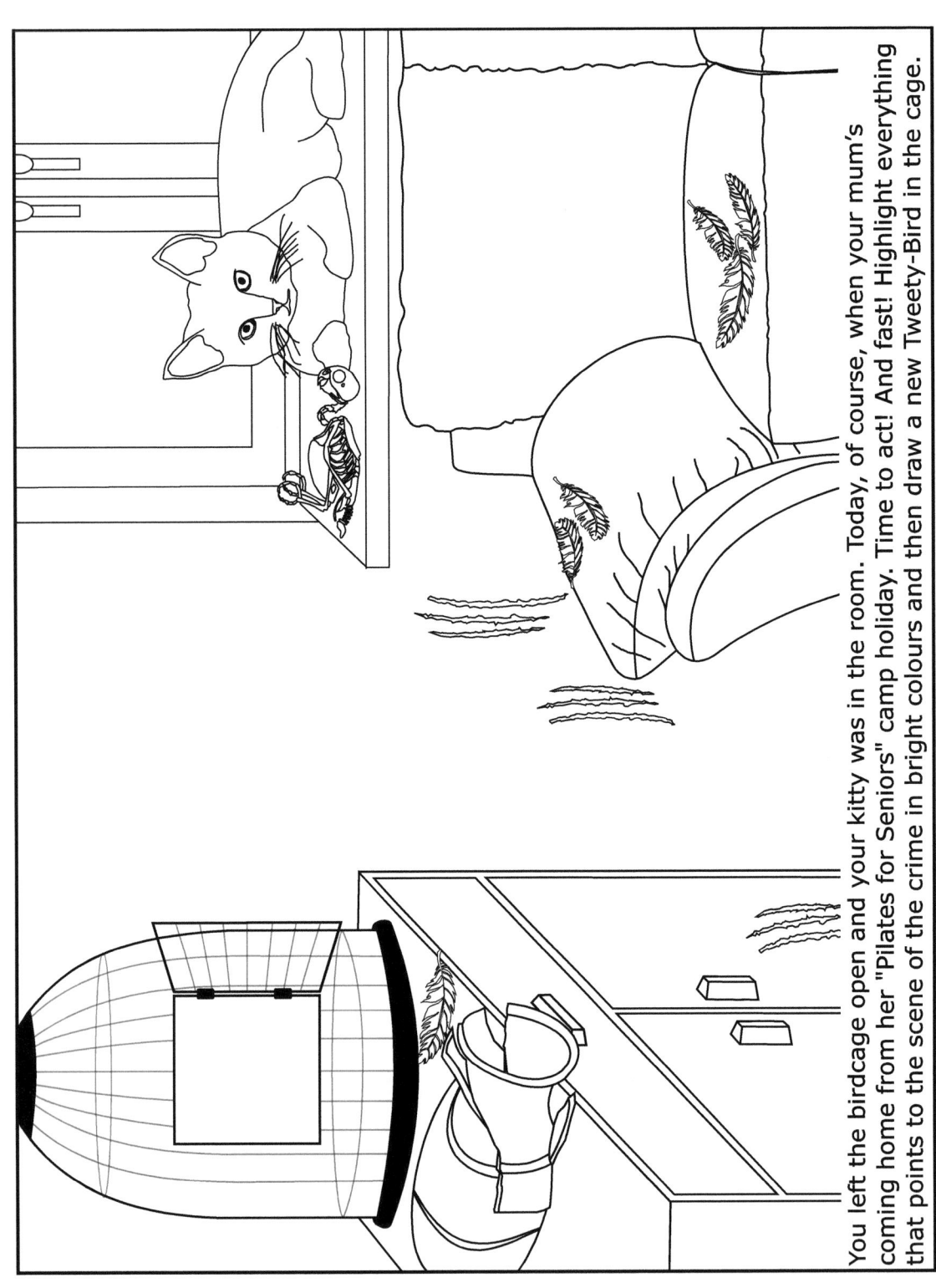

You left the birdcage open and your kitty was in the room. Today, of course, when your mum's coming home from her "Pilates for Seniors" camp holiday. Time to act! Highlight everything that points to the scene of the crime in bright colours and then draw a new Tweety-Bird in the cage.

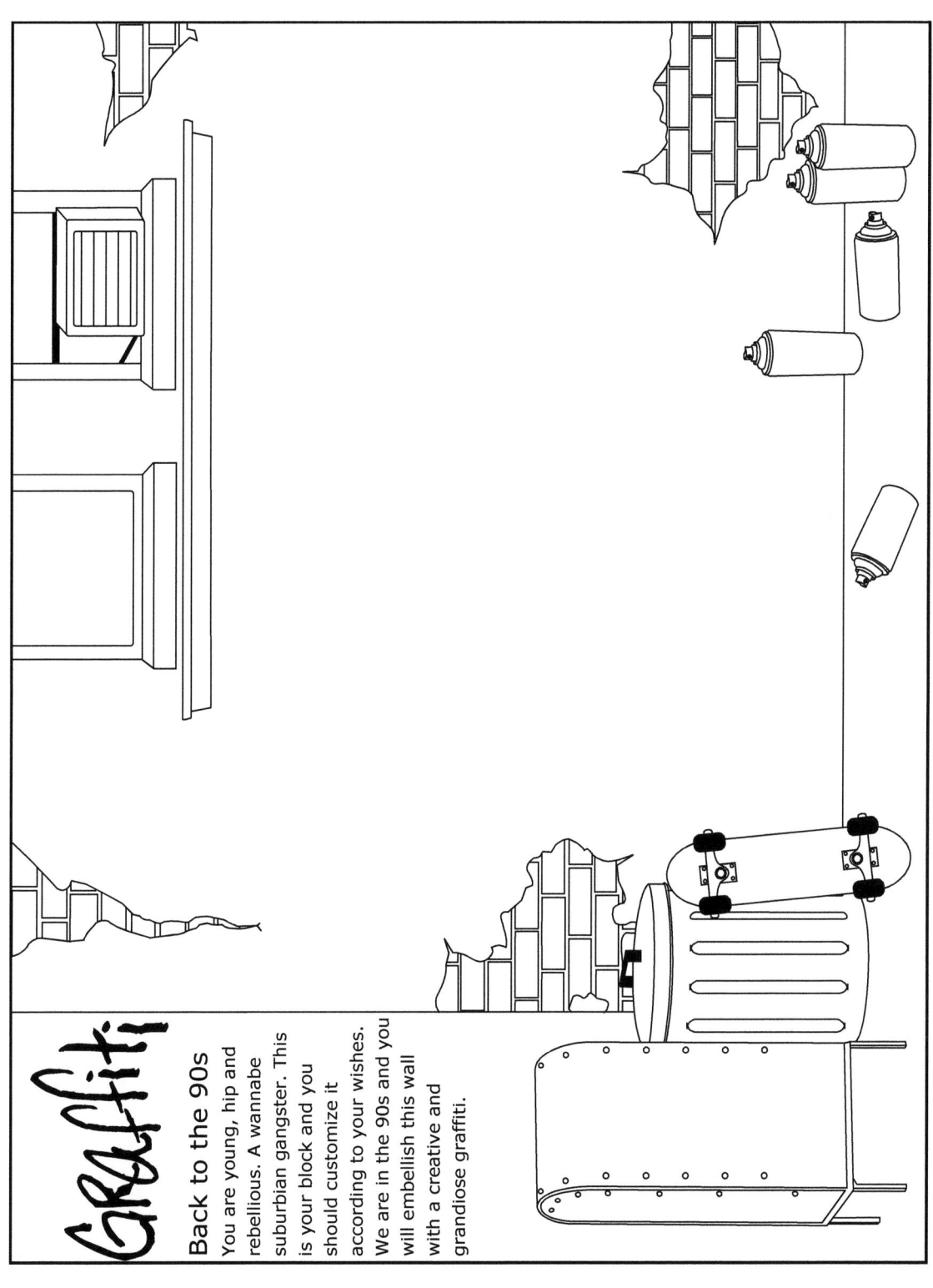

Evolution

What 5 inventions have moved us backwards instead of forwards? What new things are making us even dumber? What new things are dangerous for you and those you love? And what new things are completely unnecessary?

1. .... 2. .... 3. ....

4. .... 5. ....

It's birthday and a filled Pinata is waiting for the little Lisa.
But what's happening now? Why is her mother so shocked? Connect the dots from 1 to 94 and find it out.

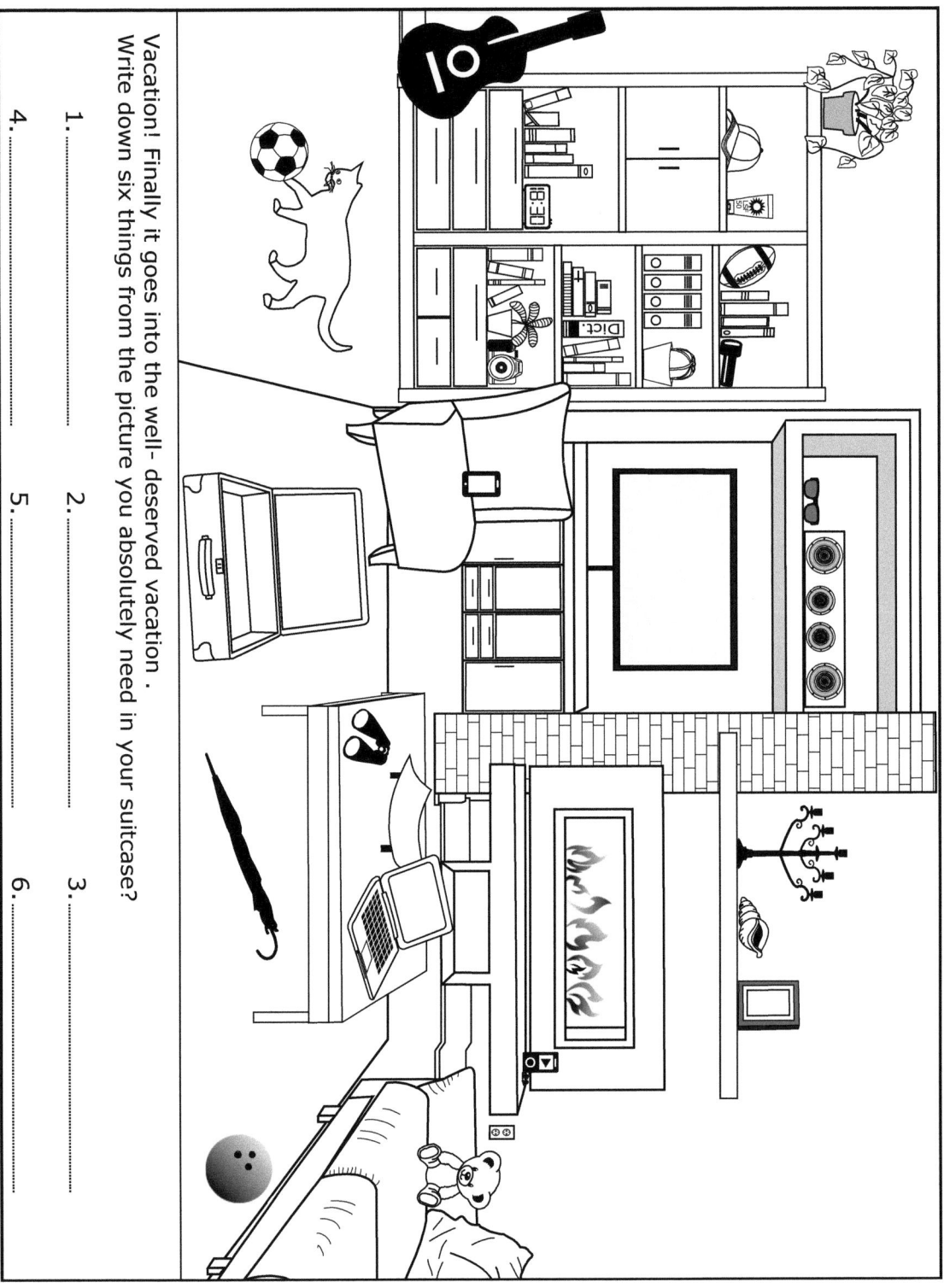

Vacation! Finally it goes into the well- deserved vacation .
Write down six things from the picture you absolutely need in your suitcase?

1. ....
2. ....
3. ....
4. ....
5. ....
6. ....

Alfred Hitchcock

Solve the rebus from left to right and complete the searched proverb.

(Solution is at the end of the book)

Color the areas with the light grey points. Use a relaxing, calming color!

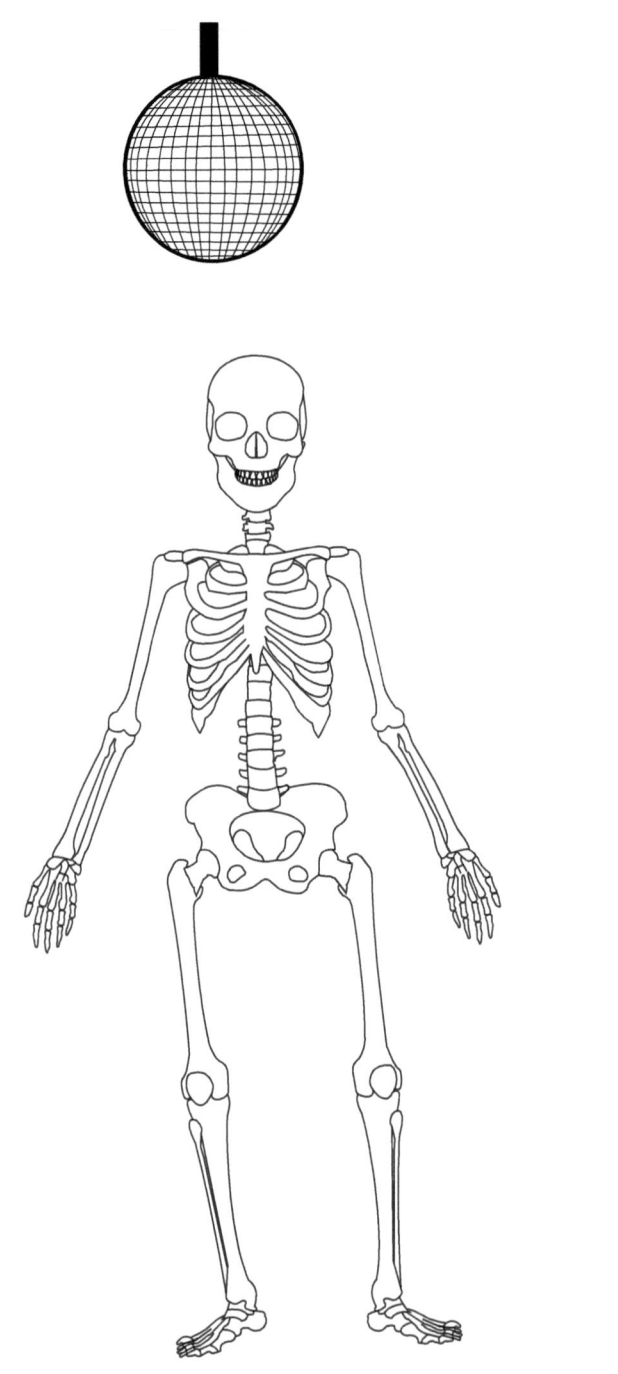

A moment ago on the skateboard and now in the disco. Draw our bony friend a cool party outfit. But he does not want to be alone. He need some incredible friends. Can you help him?

Typical man ?! Help his poor wife and draw some items into the picture which can cheer him up.

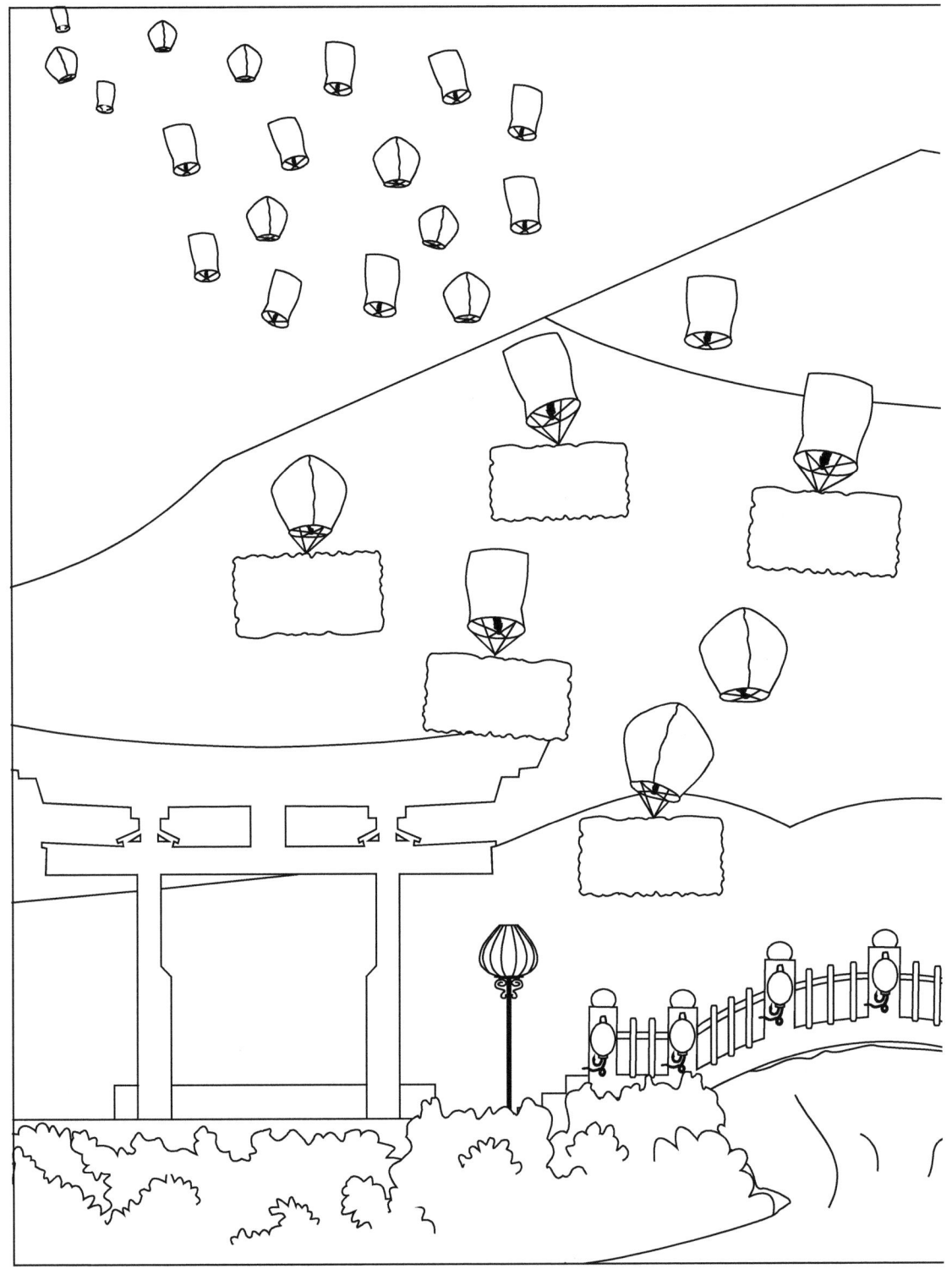

The Chinese Lantern Festival is one of the most famous festivals where Kongming Lanterns rise up to the sky. Write your deepest desires on the pieces of paper which are attached on the lanterns. If you need more lanterns don't hesitate to draw some more.

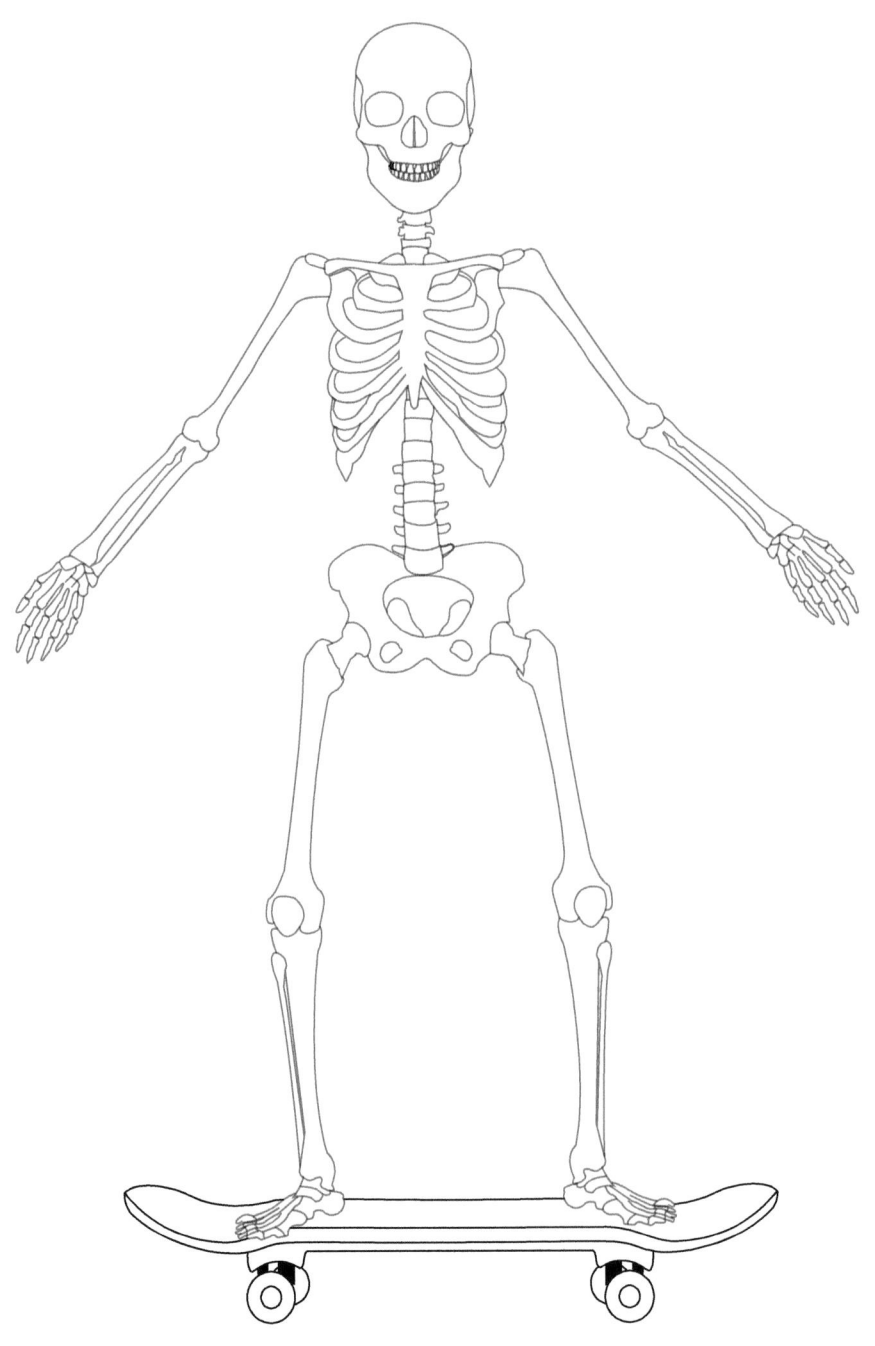

How cool is that ? A skeleton of a hipster on a skateboard ! Draw him an amazing outfit without hiding his "true self"!

That's me

name: ....

age: ....

place of residence: ....

your desired weight: ....

we know each other from: ....

When I see you, I think of...
....

For this offence, you could sue me for...
....

When I stand before the mirror, I see...
....

I would be glad to be able to repeat this one day in my life:
....

If you were my boss, I would...
....

I do this when no one is looking...
....

If we were both alone in a dark room, then...
....

Your motto:
....

Do you remember how nice it was to get people to sign your yearbook? Fill out this page and give it to a special person. Or have your favourite colleagues, your boss, your partner, or your friends fill it out.

Fill out the page according to your ideas. Draw a beautiful picture, glue on some photors, or write a dedication.

How organised are you? Draw all the objects that are in your desk drawer at work or home. Then fill in the speech bubble! What would your drawer say to you if it could talk?

If a woman in Hong Kong discovers her husband isn't being faithful, she is legally allowed to kill him but she can use nothing except for her hands.

Can you find the 10 differences between the image on the left side and this one?

(Solution is at the end of the book)

Can you remember your woman / your man of your dreams from your childhood? Now we want to see her or him. Draw your secret crush on the easel.

How much dosh finds its way into your account for the work you do each month? And how much of that do you spend on shopping? Colour in the appropriate number of mice.

S	I	A	A	N	T	T	K	E	Z	B	D	I	N
C	A	G	R	A	P	E	E	N	L	U	H	F	K
H	N	A	I	N	C	H	N	D	D	F	I	W	N
A	I	E	R	N	E	I	F	C	R	G	T	I	C
M	U	N	R	A	G	L	D	A	S	H	L	H	A
P	R	E	G	P	E	E	K	E	N	U	P	U	S
I	R	I	R	W	Z	R	R	D	Z	B	O	W	E
G	F	A	U	J	E	D	E	G	L	H	U	H	G
N	R	J	I	G	C	R	A	N	E	P	F	K	N
O	K	K	U	R	A	I	K	W	A	O	T	U	A
N	Y	O	B	E	R	T	N	A	L	N	T	I	R
I	R	M	G	G	R	D	B	L	R	D	O	G	O
S	S	O	M	D	O	O	D	N	Z	U	M	H	G
E	N	A	E	B	T	K	E	U	I	H	A	R	U
N	O	R	U	D	T	N	R	T	N	P	T	N	N
I	A	K	O	K	E	D	A	S	B	H	O	K	E
H	W	S	N	P	L	T	K	Z	S	C	N	K	E
C	Z	M	U	S	H	R	O	O	M	G	M	N	R

Find 10 fruits and vegetables and write it down on the next page of the book.

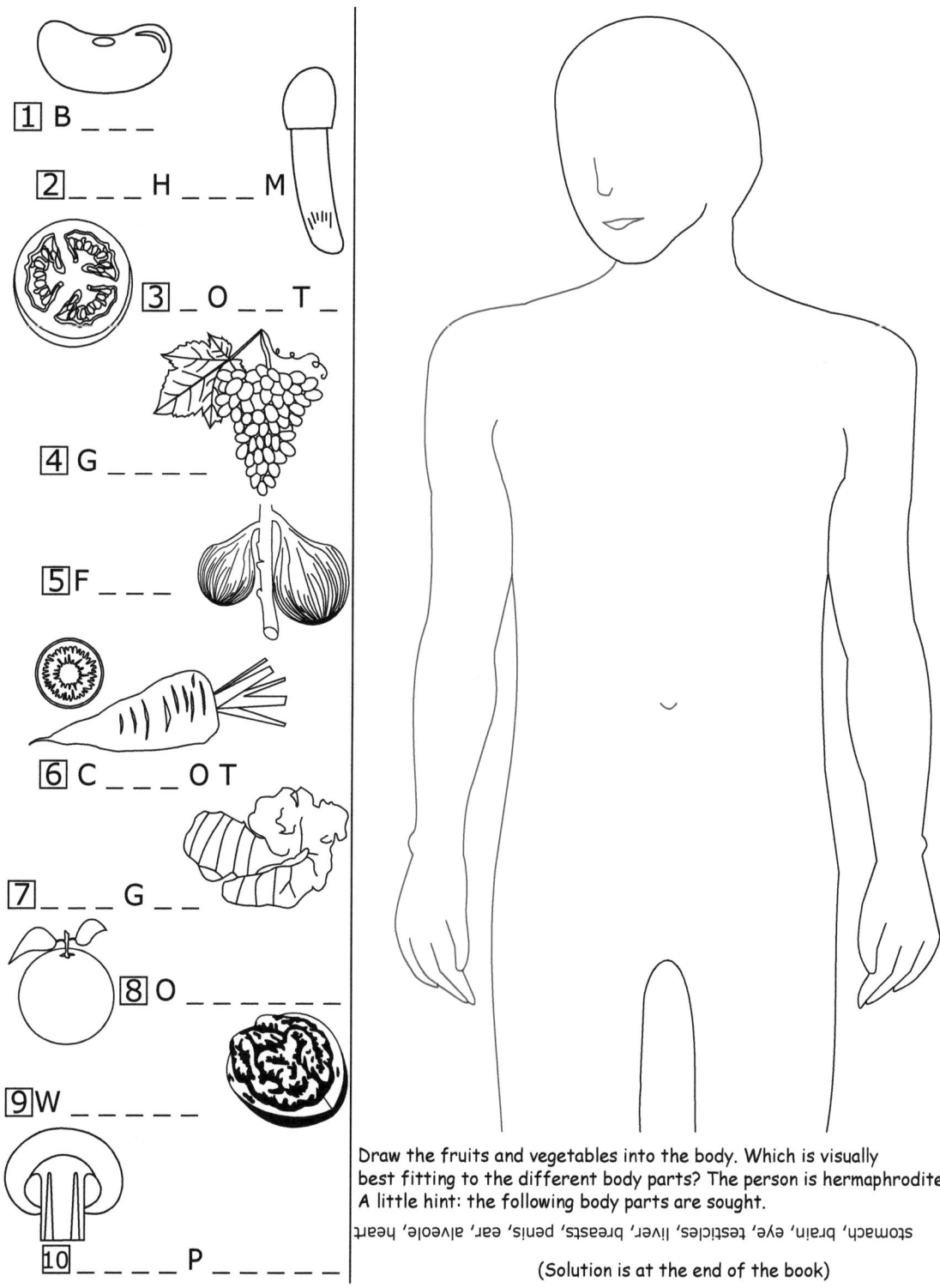

1. B _ _ _
2. _ _ _ H _ _ _ M
3. _ O _ _ T _
4. G _ _ _ _ _
5. F _ _ _
6. C _ _ _ O T
7. _ _ _ G _ _
8. O _ _ _ _ _ _
9. W _ _ _ _ _ _
10. _ _ _ _ P _ _ _ _ _

Draw the fruits and vegetables into the body. Which is visually best fitting to the different body parts? The person is hermaphrodite A little hint: the following body parts are sought.

stomach, brain, eye, testicles, liver, breasts, penis, ear, alveole, heart

(Solution is at the end of the book)

Here we go again! Somebody has crapped on the car again. Find the culprit and paint his face with red color!

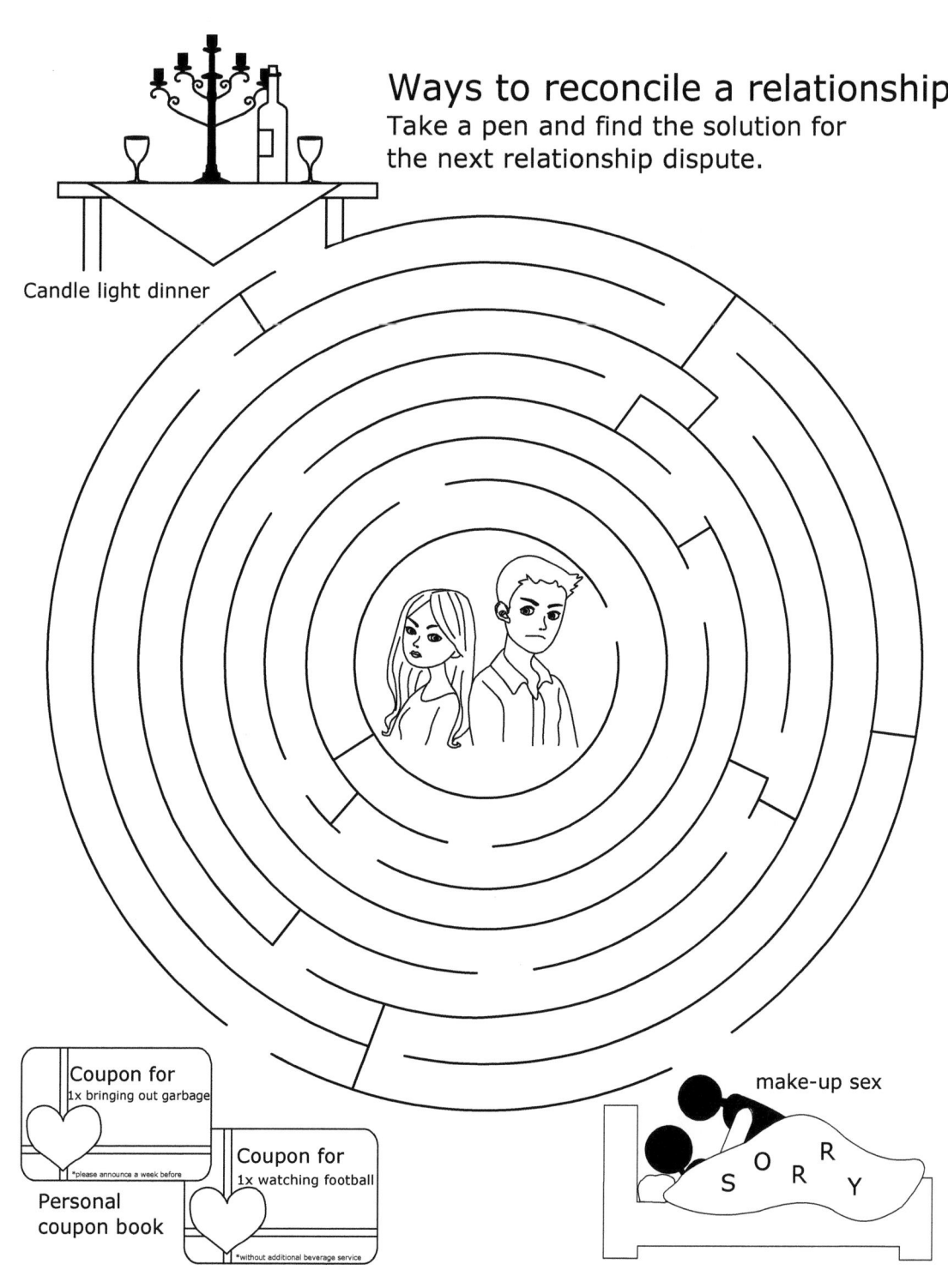

S	A	N	T	T	S	A	J	K	A	M	B	Z	P
K	F	Z	E	R	X	N	I	H	P	S	E	Y	E
A	U	S	C	E	H	A	N	A	I	M	K	H	S
N	E	T	Z	O	K	I	M	J	N	A	F	E	T
I	N	P	W	M	L	M	O	G	Z	O	T	I	O
H	M	E	Y	U	O	O	N	Z	O	S	Z	F	N
C	A	T	I	T	B	T	S	A	F	S	L	F	E
F	H	E	H	Z	U	R	N	S	X	A	T	E	H
O	Z	R	Z	R	R	T	F	F	E	H	U	L	E
L	I	S	E	G	J	I	Z	D	M	U	R	T	N
L	Y	B	M	E	K	F	T	H	L	J	M	O	G
A	W	A	M	A	H	R	T	W	L	F	K	W	E
W	G	S	O	M	A	E	H	E	E	P	I	E	M
T	H	I	P	F	L	T	B	K	R	E	O	R	N
A	A	L	L	T	I	P	I	L	S	T	D	A	I
E	Z	I	K	M	F	D	M	O	S	R	R	F	K
R	I	C	Z	L	A	H	A	M	J	A	T	U	R
G	D	A	U	M	T	S	N	G	U	B	N	J	M

Find the nine hidden sights from the opposite book page.

(Solution is at the end of the book)

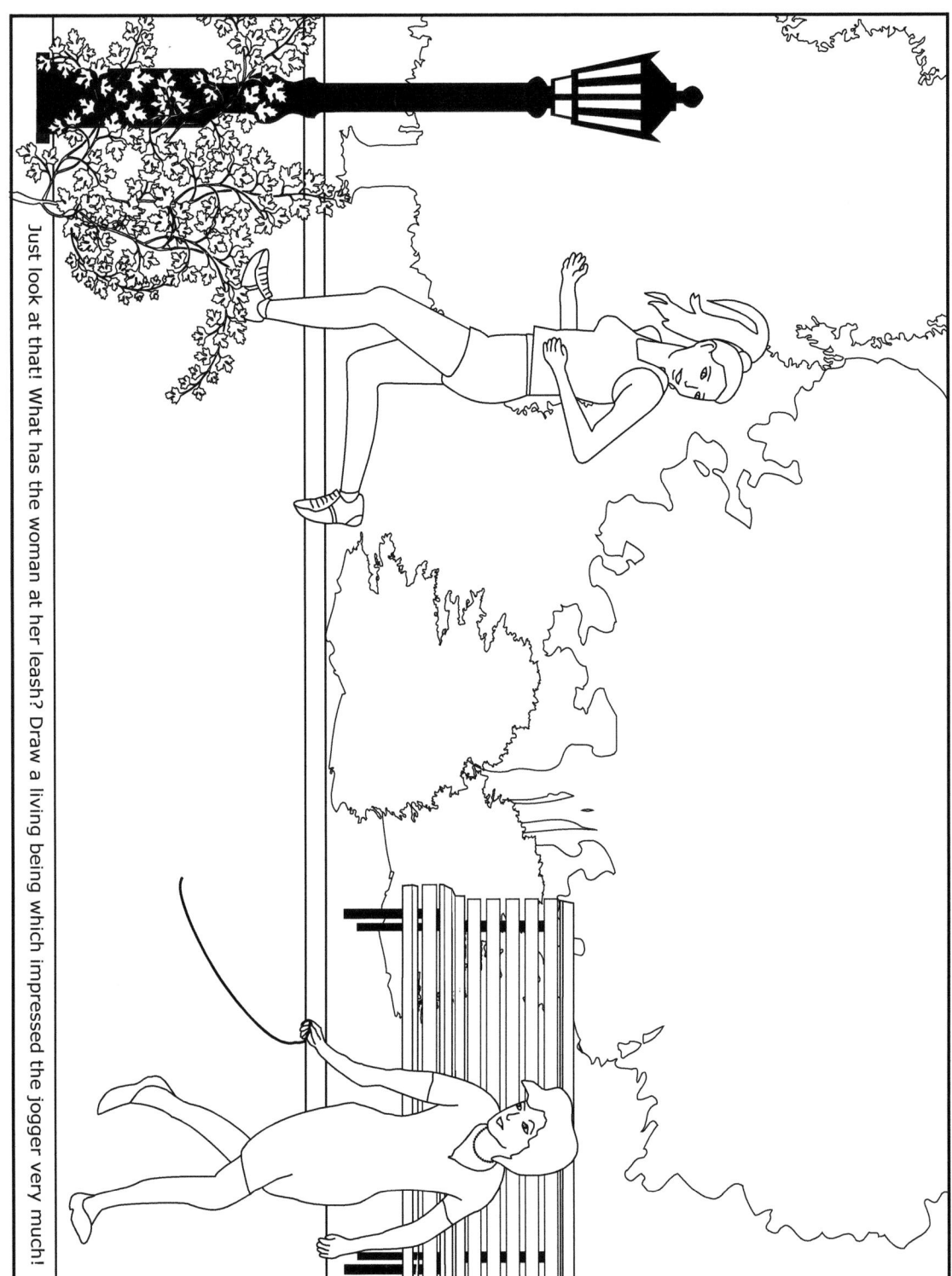

Just look at that! What has the woman at her leash? Draw a living being which impressed the jogger very much!

They've both just realised that they've forgotten their parachutes. Unfortunately, you only have 25 minutes to draw each of them a beautifully opened parachute. Will you make it and save both? Whom will you save first?

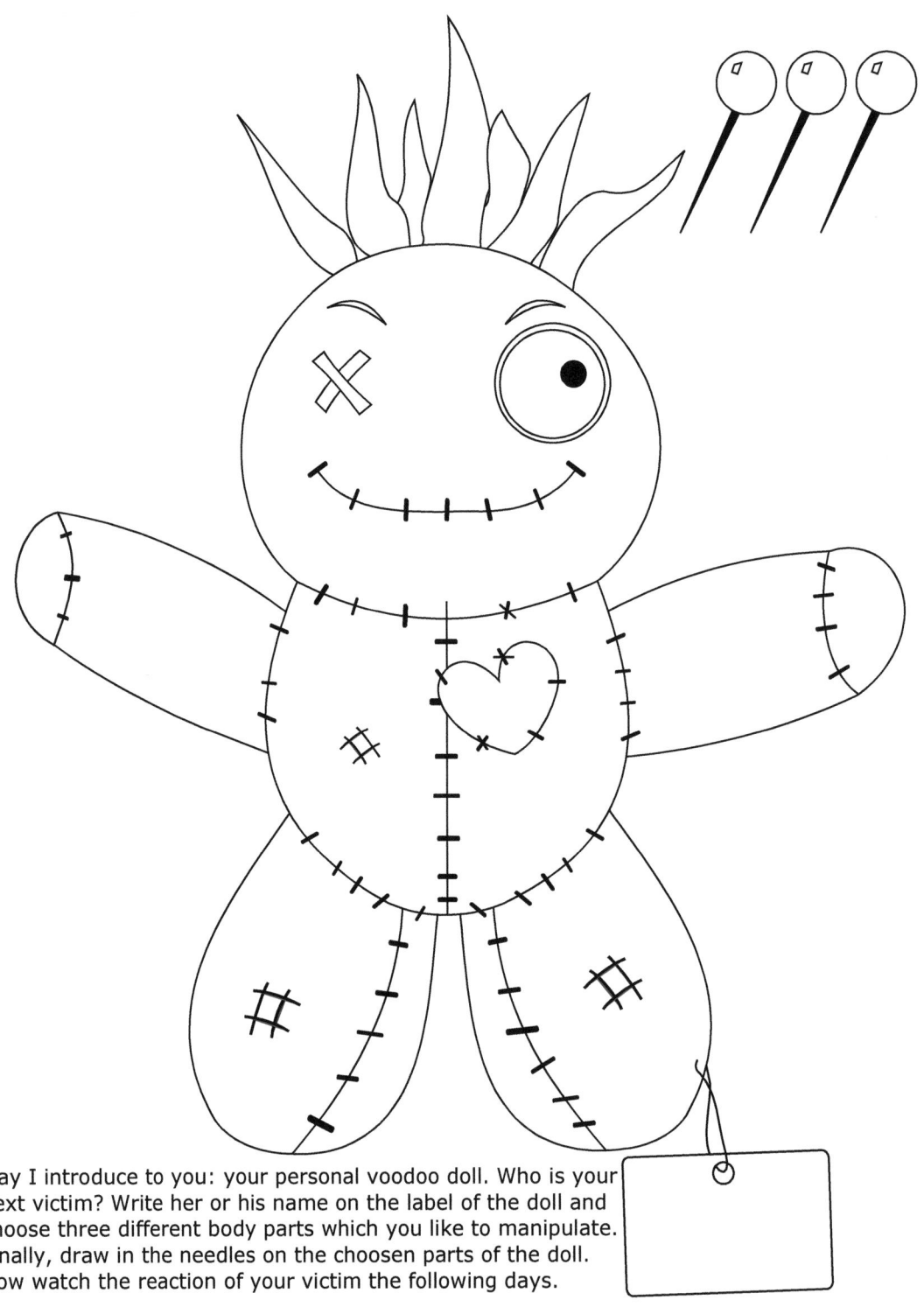

May I introduce to you: your personal voodoo doll. Who is your next victim? Write her or his name on the label of the doll and choose three different body parts which you like to manipulate. Finally, draw in the needles on the choosen parts of the doll. Now watch the reaction of your victim the following days.

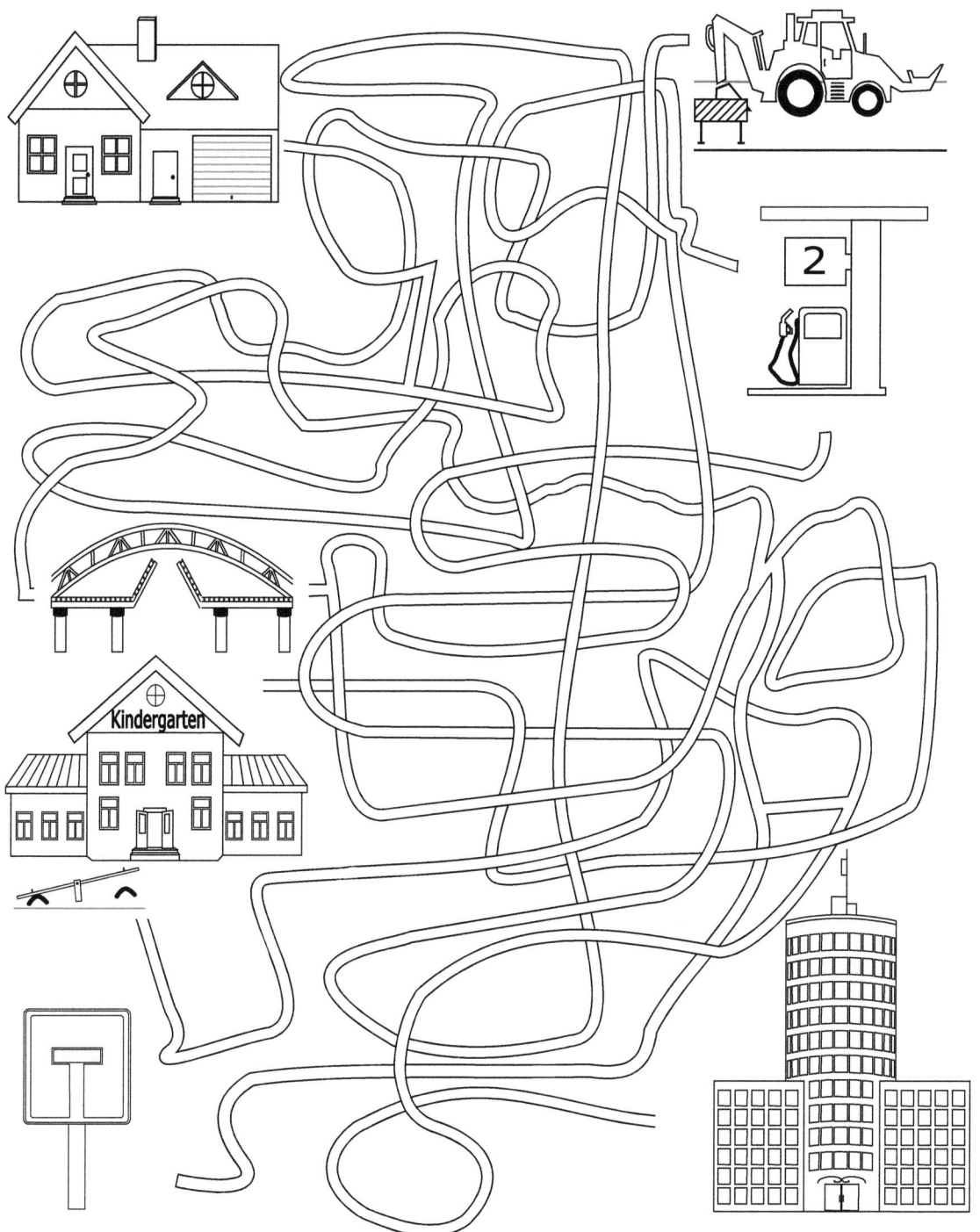

You are late! And it's your turn today bringing your kid to the Kindergarten. But thats not all. The tank of your car is empty and you have to go to the gas station. Find the right road from your home to the gas station, the kindergarten and your work as soon as possible.

Eye examination for men!

After the women have successfully resisted temptation, now it's time to test the men. Is the temptation too great or are you adamant and resist the young, naive assistant. Test yourself or your colleagues and see for yourself.

Rebus  # Solutions

feather   knide ball   hus   bandern

| The | ideal | husband |

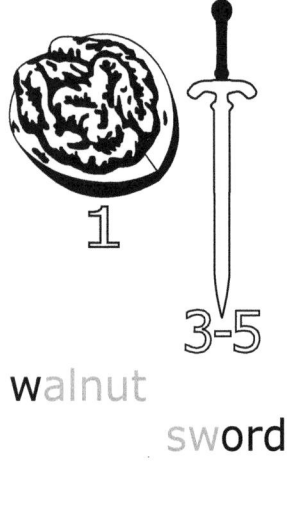

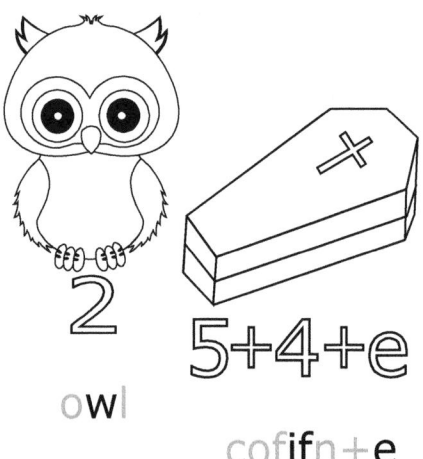

walnut sword   whistle   owl   cofifn+e

| word | his | wife |

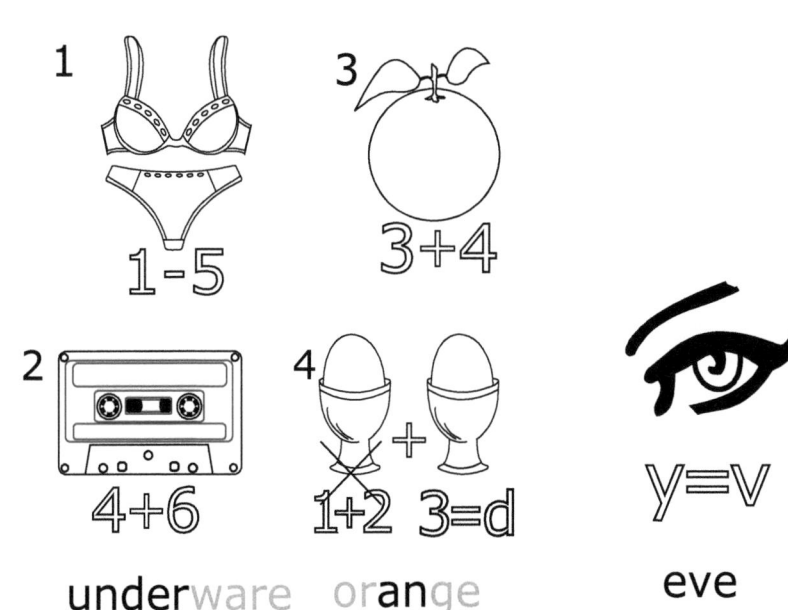

underware orange   eve   fork   fly
cassette egds

understands	every

  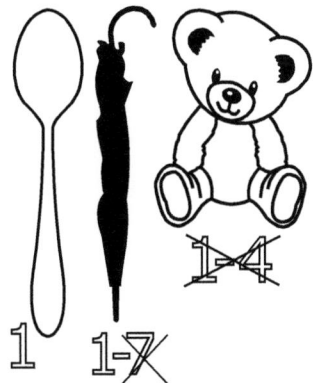

dove   shell   funnel   spoon
     ehsll   rocket   umbrella
                                                              teddy

does	not	say

Find the mistakes

Assign fruits and vegetables to the body parts!

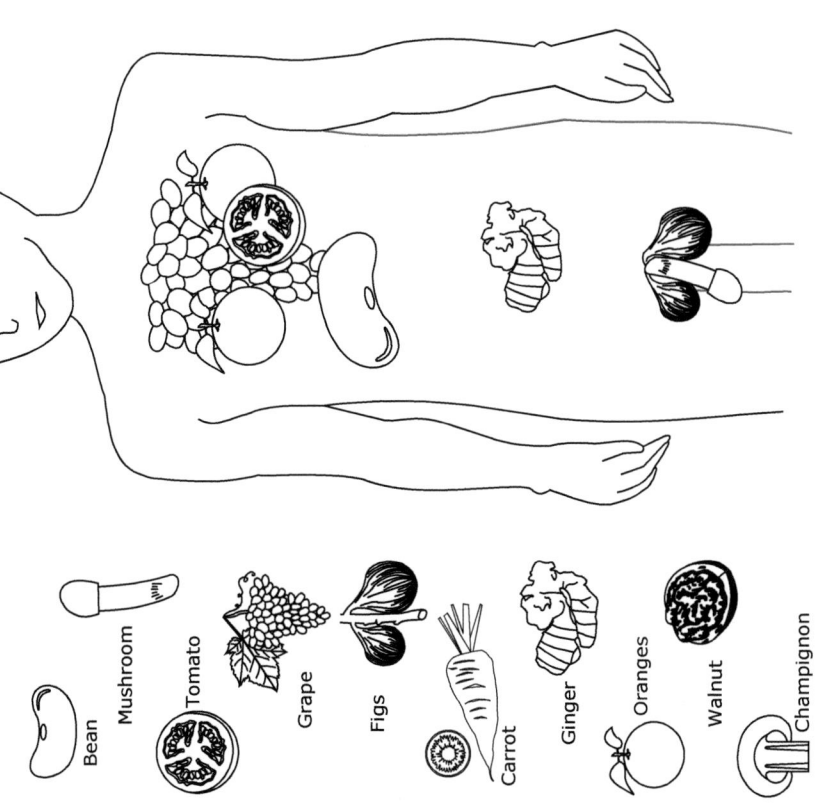

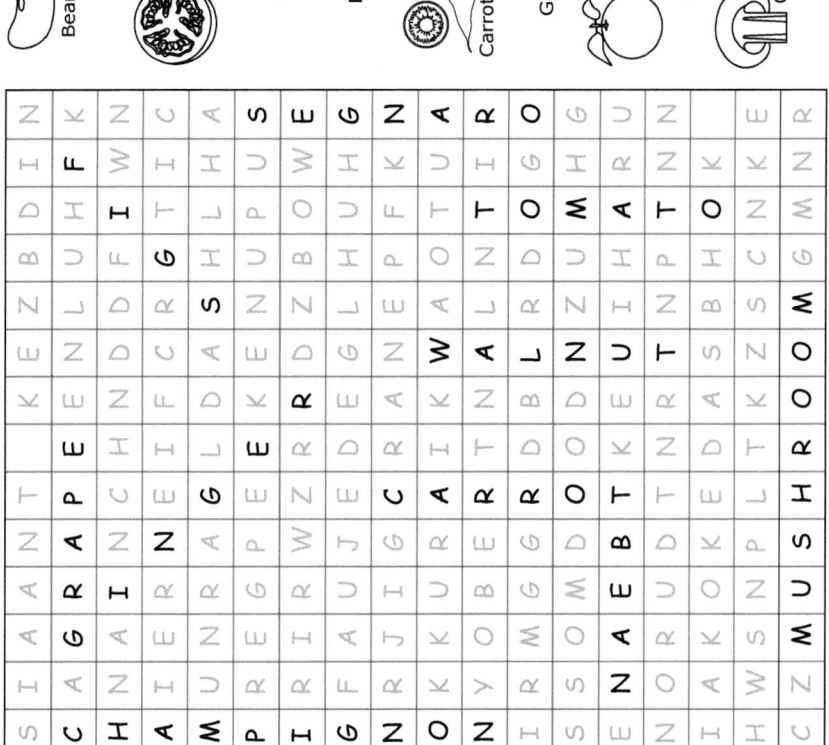

Bean=Liver; Mushroom=Penis; Tomato=Heart; Grape=Alveole; Figs=Testicles; Carrot=Eye; Ginger=Stomach; Oranges=Breasts; Walnut=Brain; Champignon=Ear

Find the hidden sights

searched terms:

- Colosseum
- Petra
- Sphinx
- Great Wall of China
- Taj Mahal
- Eiffel Tower
- Burj Khalifa
- St Peters Basilica
- Stonehenge

S	A	N	T	T	S	A	J	K	A	M	B	Z	P
K	F	Z	E	R	X	N	I	H	P	S	E	Y	E
A	U	S	C	E	H	A	N	A	I	M	K	H	S
N	E	T	Z	O	K	I	M	J	N	A	F	E	T
I	N	P	W	M	L	M	O	G	Z	O	T	I	O
H	M	E	Y	U	O	O	N	Z	O	S	Z	F	N
C	A	T	I	T	B	T	S	A	F	S	L	F	E
F	H	E	H	Z	U	R	N	S	X	A	T	E	H
O	Z	R	Z	R	R	T	F	F	E	H	U	L	E
L	I	S	E	G	J	I	Z	D	M	U	R	T	N
L	Y	B	M	E	K	F	T	H	L	J	M	O	G
A	W	A	M	A	H	R	T	W	L	F	K	W	E
W	G	S	O	M	A	E	H	E	E	P	I	E	M
T	H	I	P	F	L	T	B	K	R	E	O	R	N
A	A	L	L	T	I	P	I	L	S	T	D	A	I
E	Z	I	K	M	F	D	M	O	S	R	R	F	K
R	I	C	Z	L	A	H	A	M	J	A	T	U	R
G	D	A	U	M	T	S	N	G	U	B	N	J	M